Collins

Revised Edition

Vision 7

A Course on Values and Life Skills

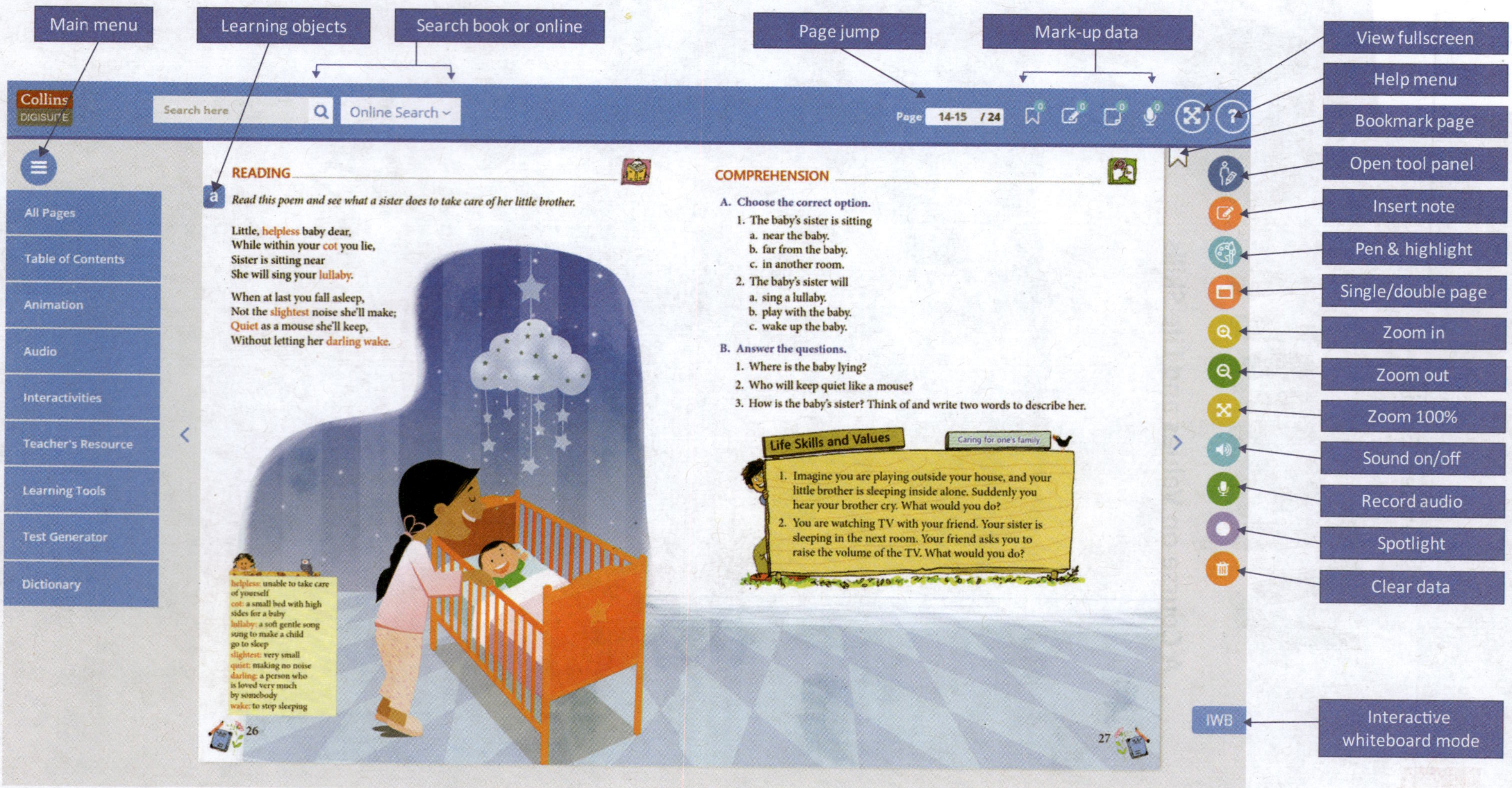

Main menu
Learning objects
Search book or online
Page jump
Mark-up data
View fullscreen
Help menu
Bookmark page
Open tool panel
Insert note
Pen & highlight
Single/double page
Zoom in
Zoom out
Zoom 100%
Sound on/off
Record audio
Spotlight
Clear data
Interactive whiteboard mode
Collins DIGISUITE
Search here
Online Search
Page 14-15 / 24
All Pages
Table of Contents
Animation
Audio
Interactivities
Teacher's Resource
Learning Tools
Test Generator
Dictionary
IWB
READING
a Read this poem and see what a sister does to take care of her little brother.
Little, helpless baby dear,
While within your cot you lie,
Sister is sitting near
She will sing your lullaby.
When at last you fall asleep,
Not the slightest noise she'll make;
Quiet as a mouse she'll keep,
Without letting her darling wake.
helpless: unable to take care of yourself
cot: a small bed with high sides for a baby
lullaby: a soft gentle song sung to make a child go to sleep
slightest: very small
quiet: making no noise
darling: a person who is loved very much by somebody
wake: to stop sleeping
26
COMPREHENSION
A. Choose the correct option.
1. The baby's sister is sitting
a. near the baby.
b. far from the baby.
c. in another room.
2. The baby's sister will
a. sing a lullaby.
b. play with the baby.
c. wake up the baby.
B. Answer the questions.
1. Where is the baby lying?
2. Who will keep quiet like a mouse?
3. How is the baby's sister? Think of and write two words to describe her.
Life Skills and Values
Caring for one's family
1. Imagine you are playing outside your house, and your little brother is sleeping inside alone. Suddenly you hear your brother cry. What would you do?
2. You are watching TV with your friend. Your sister is sleeping in the next room. Your friend asks you to raise the volume of the TV. What would you do?
27

Preface

***Vision* Revised Edition**, a course on life skills and values, is an engaging value education series meant to enable learners lead a balanced, happy and successful life. The National Education Policy, 2020 proposes the revision and revamping of all aspects of the education structure to create a new system that is aligned with the aspirational goals of 21st century education, while building upon India's traditions and value systems. It also lays focus on critical life skills and values.

Vision Revised Edition follows an interactive and multidisciplinary approach and caters to all kinds of learners with different learning styles.

Values are presented through progressively graded stories, anecdotes or poems.

Life Skills as laid down by the World Health Organization (WHO) have been covered through interesting stories.

Each book contains special chapters and colourful spreads showcasing the **United Nations Sustainable Development Goals**, which are important to achieve a just and an equitable world for all.

21st Century Skills have been mapped to each chapter with the aim of creating well-rounded individuals thriving in a constantly changing world.

Mental health and well-being of young learners is of prime importance in today's world. Therefore, **Let's Do Yoga** poster has been introduced as a brand-new feature of the book. It contains simple and doable asanas with step-by-step guidance and illustrations.

The series also focuses on mindfulness and social-emotional learning through **'happiness activities'**. Young children learn by doing, hence the series has a variety of hands-on activities, encouraging quiet reflection and sound action.

Creating a safety net for children and making them aware of **child rights** is much needed in this age and time. *Vision* Revised Edition has special advice for children through which they can face situations in which they feel afraid, pressurized or unsafe.

Vision Revised Edition comes with **Collins DigiSuite** which offers digital content packed with animated stories, slideshows and interactive activities.

***Vision* Teacher's Manuals** offer comprehensive **Lesson Plans** and **Additional Worksheets** for teachers.

In This Series ...

Vision Revised Edition adheres to the National Education Policy, 2020. Features such as 21st Century Skills, Life Skills, multiple intelligences, Sustainable Development Goals and Let's Do Yoga all align with the new policy.

Discuss

Warm-up exercise familiarizes students to the mood of the chapter

Read along

A story or a poem based on a value

Figure out

Questions based on the chapter to ensure value inculcation

Figure out

A. Tick the correct answers.

1. Albert's parents always told him that
   a. there was a big world inside the computer.
   b. there was a big world outside the computer.

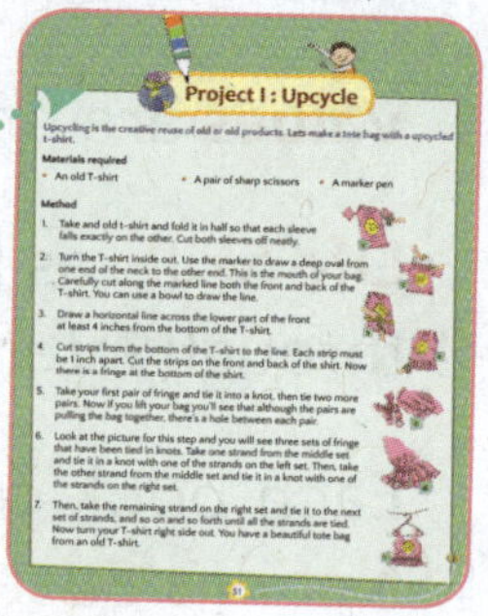

Project

Interesting projects based on the values taught

Relate

Application-based questions to check students' understanding

Relate

Tick the best options for these situations.

1. You have been gifted a parrot, but you are not interested in birds. What will you do?
   a. find out how to care for it because the parrot is your responsibility
   b. just neglect the parrot and let it become weak

Happiness Activity

Interesting activities to promote 'happiness'

Act

Interesting activities that reinforce the value taught

Remember

Brief pointers that the students can incorporate in their behaviour

Remember

- One must think of the best way to own their responsibilities.
- Shirking responsibility makes you careless.
- Certain responsibilities such as conservation of environment should be owned by everyone.
- Family responsibilities should be shared by all family members.
- When we make a choice, we have the responsibility of standing by our choice.

Think and Say

Thinking questions that encourage students to think laterally

Think and Say

You see a little puppy running in the street. It has a collar so you know it is a pet. What will you do?

Happiness Box

Enjoyable activities that promote 'happiness' and exercises based on multiple intelligences addressing different learning styles

- Musical
- Interpersonal
- Visual-Spatial
- Verbal linguistic
- Naturalistic
- Intrapersonal
- Logical Mathematical
- Bodily Kinesthetic

Child Rights and Empowerment

Useful, child-centric advice to create a safety net for children and make them aware of their rights

Sustainable Development Goals

Special chapter and a colourful spread showcasing the UN Sustainable Development Goals, a set of goals aimed at changing our world for better

Privacy and Internet Personal Safety — **Overcoming fear**

The cyber space is a source of information, knowledge and connectivity. However, it is not always a safe place to be. Access to internet means we could be interacting with total strangers or accessing unsafe content. It is imporant to understand that strangers and bullies exist in virtual world as well. We should ensure our safety while using the internet with the help of our parents or elders. It is also important to use the internet in a balanced way. Browsing the internet for excessive hours not only wastes our time but can also be bad for our health.

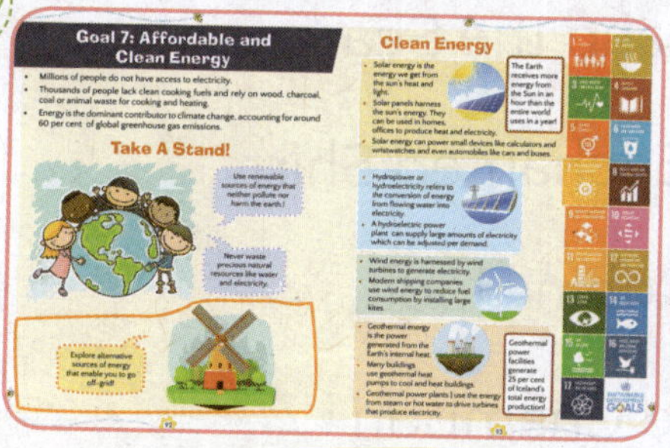

Poster

Colourful and interesting pull-out poster showcasing easy Yoga asanas

21st Century Skills

Skills necessary to succeed in the age of information: learning skills, literacy skills and social skills

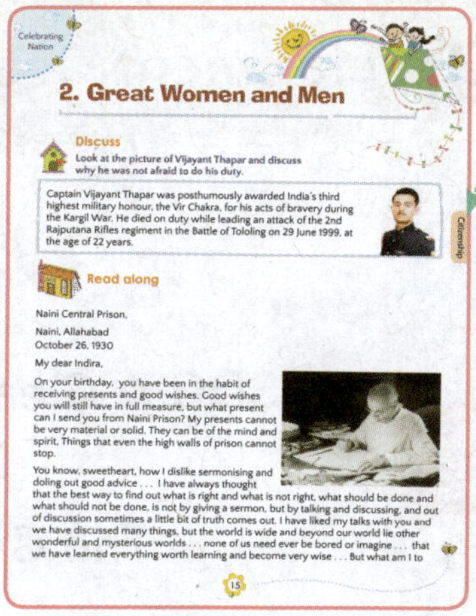

Life Skills

Chapters focusing on WHO life skills through interesting stories

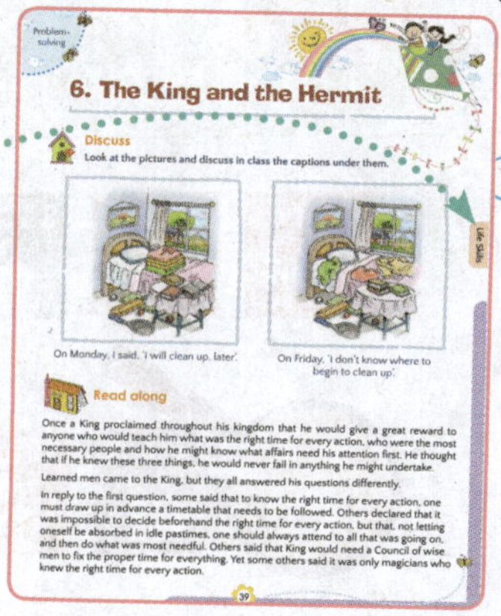

Teaching tips

- Explain why using renewable energy is important.
- Encourage students to start gardening at home as a hobby.
- Explain how using fossil uses causes climate change.

Teaching tips

Suggestions for teachers

Detailed Contents

21st Century Skills

Learning Skills	Creativity	In Spite of War
	Collaboration	Children Volunteers of Delhi
Literacy Skills	Media Literacy	Albert and Snoopy
	Cultural and Civic Literacy	Le Chambon
Social Skills	Citizenship	Great Women and Men
	Persistence	The Happy Prince
	Tolerance and Objectivity	Dorothy and the Scarecrow
	Leadership	The Enchanted Shirt
	Rights and Responsibilities	Robin Hood

Life Skills

The King and the Hermit	Problem-solving
Brave Arunima	Coping with Stress

Projects

Project I	Upcycle
Project II	Understanding Recycling
Project III	Our Unsung Heroes
Project IV	Unsung Heroes

Contents

1. Albert and Snoopy

Discuss

Read and discuss this news report in class.

News Times

DOG HERO

SUTAPA DAS

May 3, 2016

A heroic dog that helped save a sick lady from a house fire has been honoured with his name added to the Animal Hall of Fame.

Pet dog Rex received an honorary medal from pet care company, Purina Canada, after dragging the sleeping woman to the door when a huge fire broke out at the property in the Canadian province of Saskatchewan.

The loyal Alaskan Malamute German Shepherd, which had been rescued from a shelter, held on to the woman's leg, pulled her off the couch and dragged her across the room towards the front door as fire engulfed the house.

The lady said that she 'owes her life' to the brave 80 year old canine.

Read along

Albert was crazy about using computers and playing video games. He spent hours in front of the computer screen and enjoyed every minute of it. He hardly left his seat from the front of the computer. He did not go out to play. He did not have many friends. He even refused to talk to anybody in the family. His parents tried to tell him that there is more to life than computer or video games. But the more they pushed him, the grumpier he got. They told him, 'Go out Albert. There is a wide, wide world beyond your computer'.

He retorted, 'There is a very big world inside my computer. I want to know more and more about it. Let me play with my computer'.

One day, Albert came home from school. As usual, he ran to his room to be with his computer. As soon as he switched on the machine, he heard some strange noises. The noises were coming from his bedside. Cautiously, he approached the bed. He saw a little creature scratching the wooden floor. It was a small puppy. Albert could not believe his eyes. He called out to his parents. 'Am I dreaming or is that a puppy?' Albert asked them.

His mother smiled and said, 'We got this puppy for you. Do you like him?'

Albert nodded excitedly.

'Well, it is your responsibility to take care of him,' his father said.

It was certainly not easy to look after the puppy. Albert did not know what puppies eat or drink or when they sleep. So, Albert turned to his computer but not to play and game or browse. He searched all about puppies on it.

Slowly, he came to know about puppy food, puppy habits and puppy needs. Day after day, he cared for the little puppy.

He thought about changing his diet, toilet trained him and taught him new tricks. Albert gave him a name. He called him Snoopy after his favourite cartoon character.

Soon, Albert couldn't sleep unless Snoopy slept under his bed.

After school, Albert did not go to his computer. He played with Snoopy and took him for walks. Everyone, including his parents, his classmates and his teachers, enjoyed hearing Albert's stories about Snoopy. They were also impressed by his growing knowledge about pets. Albert became so involved with Snoopy that he forgot all about his beloved computer.

He now preferred to spend time with Snoopy, learn more about him and watch the way he behaved. He was happy that Snoopy was part of his world.

One day, Snoopy was missing. Albert, his parents, his teachers and neighbours looked for him everywhere, but they could not find Snoopy. They even went to the police, but Snoopy remained untraceable.

Albert was very sad. For a few days, he stayed moping in his room. His parents started worrying that he would return to his computer games and become grumpy again. To their surprise that did not happen. Instead, he told his parents, 'Can you get me another pet? Now I understand that pets are more interesting than computer games. Also, I like being responsible for them. I learned so much from Snoopy'.

Albert added, 'But don't get me a puppy'. Albert knew that nobody could replace Snoopy.

His parents were so happy that they went straightaway to the pet shop. They returned and presented Albert with a couple of gold and blue fishes in a bowl.

Albert was always found busy caring for his pets. He still used the computer but only to find out and learn more about different animals. Some of them were his pets and some were not. Every day, he discovered new things about the world of animals.

He told everyone, 'This world is a very big place. There is so much to know about it that I will never finish learning.'

Think and Say

You see a little puppy running in the street. It has a collar so you know it is a pet. What will you do?

Privacy and Internet Personal Safety

Overcoming fear

The cyber space is a source of information, knowledge and connectivity. However, it is not always a safe place to be. Access to internet means we could be interacting with total strangers or accessing unsafe content. It is imporant to understand that strangers and bullies exist in virtual world as well. We should ensure our safety while using the internet with the help of our parents or elders. It is also important to use the internet in a balanced way. Browsing the internet for excessive hours not only wastes our time but can also be bad for our health.

Remember

- One must think of the best way to own their responsibilities.
- Shirking responsibility makes you careless.
- Certain responsibilities such as conservation of environment should be owned by everyone.
- Family responsibilities should be shared by all family members.
- When we make a choice, we have the responsibility of standing by our choice.

Figure out

A. Tick the correct answers.

1. Albert's parents always told him that
   a. there was a big world inside the computer. ☐
   b. there was a big world outside the computer. ☐
2. When Albert had to look after the puppy, he
   a. searched on his computer about the habits of puppies, their food and their needs. ☐
   b. kept asking his mother for advice. ☐
3. Albert was so focused on his responsibilities for Snoopy that
   a. he forgot about his computer and only gathered information about pets. ☐
   b. he did not study and failed his exams. ☐
4. Though Albert was very sad when Snoopy went missing,
   a. he just went back to spending time with his computer. ☐
   b. he asked his parents to get him more pets. ☐
5. Albert realized that the world outside his computer is endless when
   a. he spent all his time caring for different animals. ☐
   b. he started travelling across the world. ☐

B. Albert told everyone, 'This world is a very big place. There is so much to know about it that I will never finish learning'. Do you agree with Albert? Justify your answer.

Relate

Tick the best options for these situations.

1. You have been gifted a parrot, but you are not interested in birds. What will you do?
   a. find out how to care for it because the parrot is your responsibility ☐
   b. just neglect the parrot and let it become weak ☐
2. Your toddler sister wants to accompany you to the park. You are not very happy because you will not be free to play as you like to. What will you do?
   a. quickly run to the park leaving her behind, even if she cries ☐
   b. take her along and see that she enjoys herself ☐
3. Your father has given you the responsibility of caring for the potted plants in your home. It curtails your leisure time. What will you do?
   a. water the plants for a few days and then neglect them ☐
   b. water and care for the plants daily as it is your responsibility ☐
4. Your aunt gifts you a bicycle. You like it but you dont know how to ride it. What will you do?
   a. let it remain standing in the corner of your house ☐
   b. learn to ride it and care for the bicycle because it is your responsibility ☐

Act

Be Responsible

1. Keep a basket filled with paper strips in the class.
2. Throughout the week, every time students take responsibility of some activity, such as cleaning the classroom, they write it on a strip along with their names.
3. They paste the ends to make a loop of paper strips which can go through other loops.
4. Finally, a chain of responsibilities is made for the week.
5. Display it in the school hall so that the other classes know about your responsible actions.

Happiness Box

1. **Make a Journal**

   Write about your own behaviour during the week. Write about the problems you had to face and how you handled it. Read your journals in class and let the classmates advise whether the problems could have been solved in some other way.

2. **Write an acrostic poem using the word 'Responsibility'. You may start with the first line as given below or some other line.**

Remember each day we must do a kind deed.

E ....

S ....

P ....

O ....

N ....

S ....

I ....

B ....

I ....

L ....

I ....

T ....

Y ....

Teaching tips

- Stress that responsibilities are taken up, not chosen.
- Loyalty to our responsibilities is above our own needs.
- Responsibilities towards conservation, peace and resource management should be taken up ourselves.

2. Great Women and Men

Discuss

Look at the picture of Vijayant Thapar and discuss why he was not afraid to do his duty.

Captain Vijayant Thapar was posthumously awarded India's third highest military honour, the Vir Chakra, for his acts of bravery during the Kargil War. He died on duty while leading an attack of the 2nd Rajputana Rifles regiment in the Battle of Tololing on 29 June 1999, at the age of 22 years.

Read along

Naini Central Prison,

Naini, Allahabad

October 26, 1930

My dear Indira,

On your birthday, you have been in the habit of receiving presents and good wishes. Good wishes you will still have in full measure, but what present can I send you from Naini Prison? My presents cannot be very material or solid. They can be of the mind and spirit, Things that even the high walls of prison cannot stop.

You know, sweetheart, how I dislike sermonising and doling out good advice . . . I have always thought that the best way to find out what is right and what is not right, what should be done and what should not be done, is not by giving a sermon, but by talking and discussing, and out of discussion sometimes a little bit of truth comes out. I have liked my talks with you and we have discussed many things, but the world is wide and beyond our world lie other wonderful and mysterious worlds . . . none of us need ever be bored or imagine . . . that we have learned everything worth learning and become very wise . . . But what am I to do then? A letter can hardly take the place of a talk; at best it is a one-sided affair. . . Imagine that I have made a suggestion to you for you to think over, as if we really were having a talk.

In history, we read of great periods in the life of nations, of great men and women. . . do you remember how fascinated you were when you first read the story of Jeanne d'Arc, and how your ambition was to be something like her? Ordinary men and women are not usually heroic. But a time comes when a whole people become interested in a great cause.

Great leaders have something in them which inspires a whole people and makes them do great deeds . . . In India, a great leader, full of love for all who suffer and eager to help them, has inspired our people to great actions and noble sacrifice. He has helped to make the starving, the poor and the oppressed free and happy. Bapuji is in prison, but the magic of his message has stolen the hearts of India's millions. Men and women, and even little children have come out of their little shells and become India's soldiers of freedom.

In India today, we are making history, and you and I are fortunate to see this happening before our eyes and to take some part ourselves in this great drama. What part shall we play in it?

If we are to be India's soldiers we have to respect India's honour, and that honour is a sacred trust. . . It is no easy matter to decide what is right and what is not. One little test I shall ask you to apply whenever you are in doubt. . . Never do anything in secret or anything that you would wish to hide. For the desire to hide anything means that you are afraid, and fear is a bad thing and unworthy of you. Be brave, and all the rest will follow . . . You know that in our great Freedom Movement, under Bapuji's leadership, there is no room for secrecy or hiding. We have nothing to hide. We are not afraid of what we do or what we say. We work in the sun and in the light. Even so in our private lives let us make friends with the sun and work in the light and do nothing secretly. . . and if you do so, my dear, you will grow up a child of the light, unafraid and serene and unruffled, whatever may happen.

I have written a very long letter to you. And yet there is so much I would like to tell you. How can a letter contain it?

Good-bye, little one, and may you grow up into a brave soldier in India's service.

With all my love and good wishes,

Your loving father,
Jawaharlal Nehru

Think and Say

When you salute the Indian flag every Independence Day, you feel it is not enough. True patriots' actions reflect patriotism. What will you do?

Remember

- Courage is making an honest attempt to improve situations.
- Patriotism means to contribute in every small way to your country's welfare.
- Never be afraid to do or say the right thing.
- Anything that has to be done secretively is certainly a misdeed.
- Be honest not just in words but in action.

Figure out

A. Tick the correct answers.

1. Why were Nehru's presents to his daughter not prevented by the high walls of his prison?
   a. They were birds that could fly over the walls. ☐
   b. They were gifts of the mind and spirit conveyed through written words. ☐
2. What makes ordinary men and women heroic?
   a. Great leaders who can inspire them to do great deeds and noble sacrifices. ☐
   b. The desire to win awards and rewards. ☐
3. How did Bapuji prove to be a great leader even when he was in prison?
   a. He held meetings of the prisoners. ☐
   b. People of India loved him so much that they fearlessly fought for India's freedom. ☐
4. According to Nehru, how can we judge whether something is right or wrong?
   a. If we need to hide what we are doing, it is certainly the wrong thing. ☐
   b. When people point it out to us. ☐
5. What does Nehru mean when he says that Indira must be a child of the sun?
   a. She must read every day. ☐
   b. She must not do anything secretly such that she grows up to be a child of the light, unafraid and serene and unruffled. ☐

B. **Imagine you have done something that you are scared to tell your parents about. Write a letter to your parents confessing your action.**

Relate

Tick the best options for these situations.

1. A man in your neighbourhood litters and ignores all signs that rubbish must be binned. You and your friends want to stop this. What will you do?
   a. dump rubbish in his garden at night ☐
   b. explain to him politely how his habits trouble his neighbours ☐

2. You believe that the quality of life in other countries is better than in India. What will you do?
   a. tell others patiently that own country is our home ☐
   b. join your friends and agree with them ☐

3. Your mother tells you to buy a list of things from the market and gives you the exact money for them. You want to have an ice cream. What will you do?
   a. decide to save money for the ice cream by not buying a few things in the list and lying to your mother that they were not available ☐
   b. honestly ask your mother for the money to buy an ice cream ☐

4. Your cousin who has lived in America for a few years is always complaining of how dirty your neighbourhood park is. What will you do?
   a. ask her to join you and your friends in cleaning the park on a holiday ☐
   b. join her in her complaints ☐

Act

Organize a painting competition in your neighbourhood on 'Incredible India' and share the paintings to show how people view the beauty of our country.

Happiness Box

1. **Make a list of things you want to improve about our country and write how you can improve them.**

Things I Want to Improve	Things I Can Do

2. **Have a declamation contest in your class on the topic 'Is it enough to speak like a patriot?'**

Teaching tips

- Ensure that students understand that one has to express love for one's country not through words but by doing something for it.
- Talk about the Indian freedom struggle and tell tales of ordinary men and women who participated in the freedom struggle.
- Emphasize that when you are right or doing the right thing, never be cowed down by opposition.

3. The Green Chariot

Discuss

Read and discuss in class.

Stranger than fiction.

'Tulsi gives out oxygen for 20 hours and ozone for four hours a day along with the formation of nascent oxygen which absorbs harmful gases like carbon monoxide, carbon dioxide and sulphur dioxide from the environment,' said Shyamkant Padoley, an eminent botanist.

Was this why the people of ancient India revered the tulsi plant?

Read along

The Global Goal 7, Affordable and Clean Energy, seeks to ensure access to affordable, sustainable and modern energy for all. Renewable energies are those that can be renewed or regenerated naturally. They can be used without time limit while fossil energies come from sources that will be depleted.

One hot, humid afternoon, I was standing on the pavement of the busy Rashbehari Avenue at Kolkata, when a yellow and black Ambassador cab wheezed up to me. About to dodge the traffic and clamber into it, I stopped . . . and stared. What was this? Had the cab grown a head of hair? A spiky crew cut stood on its ends! It was not even black: it was green!

I put out a hesitant hand and touched the growth covering the cab roof. O Lord! It was soft, a bit wet; it was grass! Yes. The cab had a rooftop verdant lawn. What a magical wonder!

Amazed, I went all around the cab trying to understand the phenomenon. The yellow roof supported a curved tray of a depth of ten inches that was filled with soil planted with a thick grassy mound. I pulled the door open and entered the clean interiors. The shelf behind the passenger seat was filled with potted plants. There were crotons, ferns and cacti. The dashboard held a lovely tray garden of twisted dwarf plants and pebbles in between. Only after I had my fill of this garden cab, I turned to its driver who had been watching me, all the while, with a wide smile.

'It's beautiful!' I breathed reverently. His smile just widened.

'Where to, Didi?' he asked.

'Mandevilla Gardens,' I said mechanically, and asked, 'What is your name?'

'Dhananjay Chakrabarty,' he said, 'but most people call me, Bapida.'

'Bapida you will be for me, too. But first tell how did you get such a unique idea?'

He narrated his tale.

'I have always loved plants. Wherever I live, even as a tenant, I have tried to grow plants; sometimes in a tiny patch in front of my house or in pots. One night, I discovered an empty bottle left in my cab by a passenger. Impulsively, I filled the bottle with water and placed a money plant in it and kept it on the rear window shelf of my cab. It flourished and grew roots and young, green leaves. Soon, I added more plants in my cab'. He smiled at me.

'But . . . but this grass on the roof?' I asked.

He laughed, 'Well, one day, a friend pulled my hair and said, 'What next, Bapi? Will you grow plants on your head?'

That night, I thought to myself, 'Why not? After all, the air in this city is so toxic. If I grow a garden on my cab roof, at least I will add some oxygen to the air.'

'Then?' I was eager to know more.

'First, I bought a metal sheet. Then I hired an ironsmith to fashion it into a tray with a row of tiny holes going all around its base. Once that was done, I lined it with fibre. Now that the receptacle was ready, I drove to the plant nursery. I filled the tray with pebbles, sand and clay. Finally, I planted the tray with Chinese grass. The grass took a few months to grow. We trimmed it to give a shape matching the curve of the cab roof. Finally, I mounted the tray of lush green grass on my cab roof.' he explained.

I asked the real-life hero, 'Have you faced any problems with your grassy roof?'

'None at all. In fact, my clients have often told me that the inside of my cab is as cool as that of the AC cabs.

Think and Say

You have planted some shrubs in pots and kept them on your balcony. Whenever you water them, the excess water wets the floor and you have to wipe it. What will you do?

It has been a year now that I have had this rooftop lawn. It has weathered the summer heat, the wintry cold and heavy downpours and nothing has been undone. It is flourishing just as the plants inside my cab are sprouting leaves, flowers and buds.

Bapida calls his cab the 'Green Chariot', even though he is only a hired driver of the cab. It is just that he is passionate about all kinds of plants. To him, plants breathe life and certainly they do for all of us.

'Why do people in the city of Kolkata complain about the pollution?' he asks. Giving a wide smile, he adds, 'A little greenery in every house will purify the toxic air. People say there is no space for a garden. Plants don't need much space. All they need is love. I want my Green Chariot to be an example of how space can be used to green our city.'

And I thought to myself, 'What a magnificent effort to make just a little difference! If only more people are inspired by Bapida and his Green Chariot, all these little drops would turn Kolkata into a sea of living, breathing greenery.'

If you want to contact Bapida, access the facebook page
https://www.facebook.com/people/Bapi-GreenTaxi/100008750044564

—*Sutapa Basu*

Remember

- We should try to plant as many trees as we can and take care of them too.
- If we want enough energy for everyone on the planet we are going to need to find more renewable and sustainable solutions.
- Solar energy can be used to produce electricity for lighting, heating and cooking.

Figure out

A. Tick the correct answers.

1. Bapida had lived as a tenant in several houses, yet he always
   a. grew plants in whatever little space he got as he loved greenery. ☐
   b. made them comfortable with modern amenities. ☐
2. The idea of keeping plants inside his cab came to him when
   a. the money plant in a bottle on the rear shelf of his cab flourished. ☐
   b. his friends gave him many potted plants. ☐

3. The rooftop lawn of Bapida's cab
   a. makes its driver a celebrity.
   b. keeps the cab cool and inspires people to make the city green.

4. 'The Green Chariot' is Bapida's way of telling the citizens of Kolkata
   a. that plants can make cities clean.
   b. if you grow plants on your cars, everyone will click your photographs.

5. Bapida believes pollution in Kolkata will cease to be a problem if
   a. people grew a few plants in their homes that will detoxify the air.
   b. people walked in Kolkata and did not use any kind of transport.

B. Explain why Ruskin Bond wrote, 'The thought of a world without trees became a sort of nightmare to me'.

Relate

Tick the best options for these situations.

1. You see a member of family leave the lights on even during the day. What will you do?
   a. ignore it as you don't pay the electricity bill
   b. try to make the family member aware about waste of power and how it affects our planet

2. Your friend wastes a lot of paper while drawing. She then dumps waste paper on the road. What will you do?
   a. tell your friend that paper is a plant product and should be recycled
   b. ignore the problem as you don't want to be interfering

3. You are invited to a friend's birthday. You are wondering what to take as a gift. What will you do?
   a. choose a potted plant as a gift because plants symbolize life
   b. choose an expensive artefact as you want impress your friend

4. Your mother has a vegetable garden, and she uses excess water from kitchen to water them. What will you do?

   a. not eat these vegetables because they were grown with recycled water ☐

   b. appreciate your mother for finding a way to save water ☐

Act

Eco-Activism

1. Each student must choose five households in their own neighbourhood.
2. Prepare a data sheet that gives a brief description of the families, such as the number of members and their ages.
3. Visit each of these families, talk to them about how how much electricity units do they consume. You can also try finding out how much is waste is generated everyday.
4. After two weeks make a data sheet and see the total units of power used and waste generated in five households.

Serial No.	Family Structure	Power Units Consumed	Waste Generated (In kgs)	Date
1.	4 members, father: 40yrs, mother: 35 yrs, daughter: 7 yrs, son: 5 yrs			
2.				
3.				
4.				
5.				

What do you think can be done to reduce the consumption of power in households. Make an action plan for efficient disposal of waste.

Happiness Box

Pot a Plant

1. Choose a pot with one or more holes in the bottom to allow water to flow out freely.
2. Take the soil mix that is a loose and light mixture of organic matter. Make sure it does not have weeds or insects.
3. Choose the plants taking into consideration the space they take. Don't use a small pot for a plant that might grow to be big.
4. Prepare the pots. Put a shard of broken pot over the hole(s) in the bottom of the empty pot so that the potting mix will not wash out with the water.
5. Fill the container with the soil. Pat down the soil lightly with your fingers to remove air pockets. Don't pack it down too hard.
6. To pot a plant, remove the plant from its container. Set the plant on top of the mix in the pot. Carefully fill in with small handfuls of soil.
7. Make sure the stem is completely above the surface. Leave about an inch between the soil surface and the rim of the pot. Water the potted plant a little.

2. Look at this campaign poster for the World Environment Day which is observed on 5 June every year.

Take an environment pledge and write two things you will do save energy on this day and encourage others to do.

....

....

....

Teaching tips

- Explain why using renewable energy is important.
- Encourage students to start gardening at home as a hobby.
- Explain how using fossil uses causes climate change.

4. The Happy Prince

Discuss

Read the following and discuss in class.

Athlete Milkha Singh or the 'Flying Sikh', as he is often referred to, was touted as having the potential to become India's first ever individual Olympic gold medallist. Yet despite some stellar performances at the 1958 Commonwealth Games in Cardiff, where he won gold, Singh missed the Olympic medal by a fraction of a second at Rome.

Indians were disappointed but do you agree that he did his best?

Read along

High above the city stood the statue of the Happy Prince. He was gilded all over with thin leaves of fine gold, two bright sapphires were his eyes, and a large red ruby glowed on his sword-hilt.

One night, there flew over the city a little Swallow and he alighted between the Prince's feet. His friends had gone away to Egypt, and he was following them.

Suddenly, a large drop of water fell on him. Then, another drop fell. As he looked up, he saw the eyes of the Happy Prince filled with tears and running down his golden cheeks. The little Swallow was filled with pity.

'Who are you?' he said.

'I am the Happy Prince'.

'Why are you weeping then?' asked the Swallow, 'You have quite drenched me'.

'When I was alive and had a human heart', answered the statue, 'I did not know what tears were, for I lived in the Palace of *Sans-Souci* where sorrow is not allowed to enter. My courtiers called me the Happy Prince, and happy indeed I was. So I lived, and so I died. And now they have set me up here so high that I can see all the ugliness and all the misery of my city. My heart is made of lead and yet I weep.'

The statue continued speaking in a low musical voice, 'Far away in a little street there is a poor house. Through the window, I can see a woman seated at a table.

Her face is thin and worn, and she has coarse, red hands, all pricked by the needle, for she is a seamstress. In a bed in the corner of the room, her little boy is lying ill. He has a fever. His mother has nothing to give him but river water. Swallow, little Swallow, will you not take her the ruby from my sword-hilt? You see, I cannot move.'

'My friends are waiting in Egypt,' said the Swallow.

'Swallow, little Swallow,' said the Prince, 'Will you not stay with me for one night, and be my messenger? The boy is so hungry and the mother so sad.' The little Swallow agreed to stay for one more night. 'Thank you, little Swallow,' said the Prince.

So the Swallow picked out the great ruby from the Prince's sword and flew away with it in his beak over the roofs of the town, over cathedrals, towers and the palace, the river and the ghetto. At last, he came to the house, where the boy was tossing feverishly on his bed, and the mother had fallen asleep, she was so tired. He hopped in and laid the great ruby beside the woman's thimble.

Then, the Swallow flew back to the Happy Prince. 'It is curious', he remarked, 'but I feel quite warm now, although it is so cold'. The Prince told him he felt so because he had done a good deed.

When the moon rose, the Swallow told the Happy Prince that she was flying to Egypt. The Prince asked him to stay for one more night. He told the Swallow. 'Far away across the city, I see a young man in a garret trying to finish a play but he is too cold to write any more. There is no fire in the grate, and hunger has made him faint'.

'I will wait with you one night longer', said the Swallow, who really had a good heart. 'Shall I take him another ruby?'

'Alas! I have no ruby now', said the Prince; 'my eyes are all that I have left. They are made of rare sapphires. Pluck out one of them and take it to him. He will sell it to the jeweller, and buy food and firewood, and finish his play'. The Swallow wept on hearing this, but the Prince commanded him.

So the Swallow plucked out the Prince's eye and flew away to the student's garret. The young man had his head buried in his hands, so he did not hear the flutter of the bird's wings. When he looked up, he found the beautiful sapphire. The Swallow went back to the Happy Prince and said, 'I must leave. The chill snow will soon be here.'

'In the square below,' said the Happy Prince, 'there stands a little match-girl. Her matches have fallen in the gutter and are all spoiled. Her father will beat her if she does not take home some money, and she is crying. She has no shoes or stockings, and her little head is bare. Pluck out my other eye, and give it to her, and her father will not beat her.'

'I will stay with you one night longer', said the Swallow, 'But I cannot pluck out your eye. You would be quite blind then'.

'Swallow, Swallow, little Swallow', said the Prince, 'do as I command you'.

So he plucked out the Prince's other eye, and darted down with it. He slipped the jewel into the palm of the match-girl's hand. 'What a lovely bit of glass,' cried the little girl, and she ran home, laughing.

Then, the Swallow came back to the Prince. 'You are blind now,' he said, 'so I will stay with you always.' And he slept at the Prince's feet.

The Swallow narrated the misery of the city to the Prince and leaf after leaf of gold, the Swallow picked off the body of the Happy Prince and gave to the poor. Then, the snow and frost came. The poor little Swallow grew colder and colder, but he would not leave the Prince whom he loved too well. But at last he knew that he was going to die. He had just enough strength to fly up to the Prince's shoulder once more.

'Good bye, dear Prince!' he murmured, 'Will you let me kiss your hand?'

'I am glad that you are going to Egypt at last, little Swallow,' said the Prince,

'I am going to the House of Death'. And he fell down dead at his feet.

At that moment, a curious crack sounded inside the statue. It was his leaden heart that had snapped into two.

The people pulled down the statue of the Happy Prince and melted it in a furnace. But his leaden heart would not melt. So they threw it on a rubbish heap where the dead Swallow was also lying.

'Bring me the two most precious things in the city', said God to His Angel; and the Angel brought Him the leaden heart and the dead bird.

'You have rightly chosen', said God, 'for in my Garden of Paradise, this little bird shall sing for evermore, and in my City of Gold, the Happy Prince shall praise me always.'

—Adapted from The Happy Prince by Oscar Wilde

Think and Say

You have hurt your knee while practicing for an important match that will be held tomorrow. What will you do?

Remember

- We should try to do our best to be better.
- We should make the effort to be part of the solution and not the problem.
- Always give credit to the person who deserves it.
- We should keep practising our skills till we are good.
- We should only make promises that we can keep.
- We should try our best to make a difference and inspire others to do the same.

Figure out

A. Tick the correct answers.

1. Why was the golden statue of the Prince crying?
   a. The Prince was sad to see the ugliness and misery of his city. ☐
   b. The Prince wanted to go to Egypt with the Swallow. ☐

2. Why did the Swallow stay the first night and not go to Egypt?
   a. He wanted to enjoy the city life. ☐
   b. He felt sorry for the seamstress and wanted to help her. ☐

3. Why did the Swallow decide to stay with the Prince even though it was getting very cold?
   a. The Swallow was too kind to leave the Prince. ☐
   b. The Swallow was happy with the Prince as he kept him warm. ☐

4. Why did the Prince's heart break when the Swallow died?
   a. The Prince's heart was too old. ☐
   b. The Prince's heart could not tolerate the sorrow of the Swallow's sacrifice. ☐

5. Why did the Angel think that the dead bird and the broken heart of the Prince were the two most precious things on earth?
   a. They had no time to search for really precious and expensive things. ☐
   b. The bird and the heart of the Prince held infinite love and kindness. ☐

B. Between the Prince and the Swallow, whose sacrifice do you consider greater?

Relate

Tick the best options for these situations.

1. Your teacher is making the entire class practise rock climbing. It is tough, and many students are close to giving up. What will you do?
   a. also give up though you have the energy to climb to the top ☐
   b. use all your strength to reach the top because you believe in yourself ☐

2. You have been studying the whole day for an important test. By night you are tired

but you have three chapters. What will you do?

a. push yourself and make the effort to study those chapters ☐

b. leave the chapters and go to sleep ☐

3. There are just two minutes to the end of the football match, and you are extremely tired. The ball is passed to you, and you have a chance of scoring the winning goal. What will you do?

a. make a half-hearted effort and miss the goal ☐

b. use all your strength and score the winning goal ☐

4. You have to tidy your room before going to play. What will you do?

a. take time to completely clean and tidy every corner of your room ☐

b. stuff your cupboard with all the dirty clothes, books and toys ☐

Act

They Do Their Best for Our Best

Adopt one helper in your school without whom your school will not be the clean, organized place to learn and enjoy that it is.

Take a week to learn about the helper and his or her family. If possible, try to visit the helper's family. Take some photographs with the helper, his or her family or while at work. Make a PowerPoint presentation about the helper and share in your class.

Happiness Box

1. Let's Converse Better

Make a chart on 'How to Converse Better'. Include some of the following tips and add more of your own ideas. Decorate it with artwork and stickers. Share it in your class.

How to Converse Better

1. Talk respectfully, taking care to maintain the dignity of the person being spoken to.
2. If there is a difference of opinion, agree to disagree.
3. Respect the views that others hold.
4. Accept differences and identify commonalities.

....

....

2. **Choose a group of students in school younger to you. Take out time during the school recess or an activity period to tell the group the story of 'The Happy Prince'. Remember that you have to tell the story not read it. Then, invite questions from the students and have a group discussion about 'Doing one's best'.**

Teaching tips

- Emphasize that genuine help is extended without any expectation. False gestures can mislead people.
- Remind students that a good deed always returns to the doer in some way or the other.
- You come closer to people and make true friends when you express your feelings for them from your heart.

5. In Spite of War

Discuss

Look at the pictures and discuss in class what makes the little girl happy or unhappy.

Hope is eternal.

Read along

In spite of war, in spite of death,
In spite of all man's sufferings,
Something within me laughs and sings
And I must praise with all my breath.
In spite of war, in spite of hate
Lilacs are blooming at my gate,
Tulips are tripping down the path
In spite of war, in spite of wrath.
"Courage!" the morning-glory saith;
"Rejoice!" the daisy murmurth,
And just to live is so divine
When pansies lift their eyes to mine.
The clouds are romping with the sea,
And flashing waves call back to me
That naught is real but what is fair,
That everywhere and everywhere
A glory liveth through despair.

Though guns may roar and cannon boom,
Roses are born and gardens bloom;
My spirit still may light its flame
At that same torch whence poppies came.
Where morning's altar whitely burns
Lilies may lift their silver urns
In spite of war, in spite of shame.
And in my ear a whispering breath,
"Wake from the nightmare! Look and see
That life is naught but ecstasy
In spite of war, in spite of death!"

—Angela Morgan

Think and Say

Your brother has been hurt and his leg is in plaster. He is very sad that he is unable to run about. You want to cheer him up. What will you do?

Remember

- Peace is necessary for success and prosperity.
- We must learn to live in peace with each other and with nature.
- When we send out thoughts of goodwill in difficult times, there will be peace.
- We have to remain calm within to bring peace outside.
- When everyone decides to do the right thing irrespective of selfish needs, there will be peace.
- War cannot solve problems that peace can.

Figure out

A. Tick the correct answers.

1. Though people are suffering due to war, the poet
   a. feels happiness rising inside her.
   b. feels anger bubbling inside.
2. People are dying and there is anger everywhere. Yet Nature seems to say
   a. be courageous because new life is like flowers that bloom.
   b. regret what is lost because it never comes back.
3. There is war amongst countries while Nature
   a. adds more unhappiness to the world.
   b. fills the world with beauty and glory.
4. Nature's message to humanity is
   a. war is the solution to end conflicts of the world.
   b. colour your emotions with joyous beauty of flowers around you.
5. The poet wants to stress that
   a. hope is eternal and all sorrows pass with time.
   b. it is impossible to recover from losses.

B. Explain what the poet means by these words.

'My spirit still may light its flame

At that same torch whence poppies came.

Where morning's altar whitely burns

Lilies may lift their silver urns

In spite of war, in spite of shame'.

Relate

Tick the best options for these situations.

1. Your friend has failed the final exams for class seven. He feels he can never progress in life. What will you do?
   a. agree with him and pull a long face to discourage him ☐
   b. urge him to pull himself out of self-pity and start studying ☐

2. You have fractured your leg and your doctor has asked you to curtail outdoor games for sometime. What will you do?
   a. play indoor games like chess ☐
   b. mope around the house and watch silly programmes on TV ☐

3. Your brother accidently breaks an expensive glass vase. What will you do?
   a. scold him for his carelessness ☐
   b. express relief that your brother is not injured by the broken glass ☐

4. You had planted flowers in the garden putting in a lot of effort. Your brother lets in a goat by mistake and it eats the flowers. What will you do?
   a. clean up the half-eaten garden and tell yourself that the flowers will bloom again ☐
   b. scold your brother ☐

Act

Each student can make a My Wish for Peace banner. It can include the peace symbols, doves and their wish for peace. They can even write their wish on a cardboard cut-out of a dove. Share all the wish banners in class.

Happiness Box

1. Make and exchange with friends a Hope for Peace bookmark with a message.

Method

- Cut out your bookmark from a stiff white cardboard paper of rectangular shape, 5 × 2 inches.
- Taper or arch one end of it with scissors.
- Punch a hole in the top half of that end and pass through it a colourful string or ribbon to act as a marker when the bookmark is used.
- Write the above message on one side and 'Hope for Peace' on the other side.
- Decorate the bookmark and gift it to your friend.

2. Lets Learn the Tune

Listen to the song 'I Have A Dream' sung by the music group ABBA. Copy the lyrics and learn the tune.

Form three teams in your class. Each team will sing one stanza of the song. Then, the entire class can sing the complete song.

Teaching tips

- Emphasize on the importance of maintaining a positive attitude despite all problems.
- Reiterate the truth that everything, both bad and good times, are temporary and will soon pass.
- Tell them stories of how dealing patiently with obstacles in life and retaining hope has been the ladder to success for many renowned achievers.

6. The King and the Hermit

Discuss

Look at the pictures and discuss in class the captions under them.

On Monday, I said, 'I will clean up, later'.

On Friday, 'I don't know where to begin to clean up'.

Read along

Once a King proclaimed throughout his kingdom that he would give a great reward to anyone who would teach him what was the right time for every action, who were the most necessary people and how he might know what affairs need his attention first. He thought that if he knew these three things, he would never fail in anything he might undertake.

Learned men came to the King, but they all answered his questions differently.

In reply to the first question, some said that to know the right time for every action, one must draw up in advance a timetable that needs to be followed. Others declared that it was impossible to decide beforehand the right time for every action, but that, not letting oneself be absorbed in idle pastimes, one should always attend to all that was going on, and then do what was most needful. Others said that King would need a Council of wise men to fix the proper time for everything. Yet some others said it was only magicians who knew the right time for every action.

Equally varying were the answers to the second question. Some said, the people the King most needed were his councillors; others, the priests; others, the doctors; while some said that warriors were the most necessary.

To the third question, as to what was the most important thing for him to do. Some said science, others said skilled warfare and yet others said religious worship.

Since all the answers were different, the King decided to give the reward to none. He decided to consult a hermit for the right answers.

The hermit lived in the woods and he received nobody but common folks. The King put on simple clothes and walked alone to the hermit's hut.

When the King approached, the frail hermit was digging the ground in front of his hut. The King went up to him and said, 'I have come to you, wise hermit, to ask you to answer three questions. These are: How can I learn to do the right thing at the right time? Who are the people I most need, and to whom should I, therefore, pay more attention than to the rest? And, what affairs are the most important and need my first attention?'

The hermit listened to the King, but said nothing. The King offered to help the hermit in his digging.

'Thanks!' said the hermit. Giving the spade to the King, he sat down on the ground.

When he had dug two beds, the King repeated his questions. The hermit again gave no answer, but rose, stretched out his hand for the spade, and said, 'Now you rest and let me work a bit'.

But the King did not give him the spade and continued to dig till sunset. Then the King asked the hermit, 'Will you answer my questions or shall I return home?'

'Here comes someone running', said the hermit, 'Let us see who it is'.

The King turned around and saw a bearded man come running out of the woods with his hands pressed against his bleeding stomach. He fell fainting on the ground moaning feebly.

The King and the hermit unfastened the man's clothing. The King washed the wound and bandaged it with his handkerchief. Then, he kept changing the bandage. When the bleeding stopped, the wounded man asked for a drink of water. The King brought fresh water for him.

He carried the wounded man into the hermit's hut and laid him on the bed. The King was so tired that he crouched down on the threshold and fell asleep. In the morning when he awoke, he saw the wounded man looking at him.

'Forgive me!', said the bearded man in a weak voice.

'I do not know you and have nothing to forgive you for,' said the King.

The man said, 'You executed my brother and seized his property. I was angry and wanted to kill you. I waited to ambush you on your return from the forest. When you did not return, I came out to search for you. Your bodyguards saw me and attacked me. But you saved my life'.

He was ashamed of himself. He begged the King, 'Forgive me. I promise to serve you till the end of my days'.

The King was very glad to have made peace with his enemy so easily and promised to send physicians to cure him as well as give him back his property.

The King then approached the hermit and again asked for the answers to his three questions.

'You have already received the answers!' said the hermit.

'What do you mean?' asked the King.

Think and Say

You have a lot of homework to complete. But there is a cricket match you want to play in the evening. You can finish your homework before playing or after playing. But playing will tire you out. What will you do?

'Don't you see', replied the hermit. 'If you had not pitied my weakness yesterday, and had not dug for me the whole day, that man would have attacked you, and perhaps killed you. So the most important time, then, was the time you were digging, I was the most important man and to help me was your most important business. Afterwards when that man ran to us, the most important time was when you were attending to him, for if you had not bound up his wounds, he would have died without having made his peace with you. So he was the most important man, and what you did for him was your most important business. Always remember: there is only one time that is important– Now! It is the most important time because it is the only time when we have any power. The most necessary man is he with whom you are at that time, and the most important work is to help or listen to that man, since he is there with you in that moment.

—Adapted from a story by Leo Tolstoy

Remember

- Only when time is planned, can it be best utilized.
- The most important time is now and the most important action is one that you need to do now.
- The most important action is the one that you do now.
- Every time you put off an action, it loses its utility.

Figure out

A. Tick the correct answers.

1. If the King knew the right time for action, the right person and the most important action, he would
   a. be successful in anything he did. ☐
   b. become the wisest of all men. ☐
2. When the King asked the hermit his question, the hermit remained silent because
   a. he did not know the answers. ☐
   b. he knew that the King would get his answers through the day's events. ☐
3. When the King saw the bleeding man, he
   a. immediately bandaged his wound and cared for him. ☐
   b. ignored the man and kept on digging the beds. ☐
4. The wounded man asked the King to forgive him because
   a. he had intended to kill the King who helped and cared for him. ☐
   b. he did not recognize the King. ☐
5. The most important time is the present time because
   a. we can only enjoy happiness in the present time. ☐
   b. we have control over our actions, words and choices during the present time. ☐

B. If the King had returned home because the hermit did not answer his questions, the story could have ended differently. Write a different ending to the story.

Relate

Tick the best options for these situations.

1. You want your father to bake a cake for your friends who are visiting you in the evening. He asks you to buy for him some of the ingredients in the morning. What will you do?
   a. tell him you will do it later as you are busy with your own work ☐
   b. immediately shop for your father so that he can start baking ☐

2. Your mother requests you to help her wash the car on a Sunday morning. Your friends are waiting for you to join them on a cycling trip. What will you do?
   a. tell your friends to wait or ask them to join you in washing the car ☐
   b. tell your mother you cannot help as your friends are waiting ☐

3. Your project partner wants to work on a project. You are feeling lazy. What will you do?
   a. tell your partner you will work on the project the next day ☐
   b. ignore your laziness and sit down to work on the project ☐

4. Your younger brother has to write a poem and submit it for the school magazine next morning. He asks you to help but you are watching TV. What will you do?
   a. switch off the TV and help your brother ☐
   b. make excuses and tell him to work on it himself ☐

Act

Win a Card Contest

Materials required

- Several decks of playing cards
- Stopwatch

Method

1. Divide the class into several teams. One student must time the contest with a stopwatch.
2. Each team gets a deck of playing cards that has to be laid out in a specific manner given below. No card must touch any other card.
3. Each team can do a trial run and then give an estimated time to finish the pattern. Remember, to win not only will your team have to finish within the estimated time, but have the shortest time among all the teams. The pattern is given here.

♥	A	5	J	9	2	Q	10	7	3	8	K	4	6
♠	A	5	J	9	2	Q	10	7	3	8	K	4	6
♦	A	5	J	9	2	Q	10	7	3	8	K	4	6
♣	A	5	J	9	2	Q	10	7	3	8	K	4	6

Happiness Box

1. **Personal Monthly Planner**

Materials required

- Printout of the calendar months of the year
- 12 × 12 inches chart paper for each month
- Post-it™ sets
- Colour pens

Method

1. Print dates and days of each month.
2. Use the printout to make a planner for each month on the chart paper cutouts.
3. On the planner, stick Post-it™ tags in one colour for all scheduled study times, in another colour for all scheduled fun activities.
4. Once you complete the monthly planner, you will see that you have planned out everything that you have to do and ought to do in a month.
5. Put the planner up in your room and consult it every day. Change the planner every month.

2. **Find out when the TV programmes are aired.**

Form pairs. Each of you pick up one of the incomplete TV programme cards given below. Ask each other questions to complete your card.

Nos	Name of the TV Programme	Time	Day
1.	Archie and Friends	6.00 pm	
2.			Tuesday
3.	News Round Up		Monday
4.		11.30 am	

Nos	Name of the TV programme	Time	Day
1.			Wednesday
2.	Dinosaur World	5.30 pm	
3.		8.00 am	
4.	Travel the World With Me		Sunday

Teaching tips

- Reiterate that time once lost can never be gained.
- Explain how procrastination has been disastrous for most people.
- Help students sort out the important things from the unimportant things in life. There is no time like 'now' to do what you want to, so make the best of it.

Happiness Activity

Nature has a direct and positive impact on our happiness. There is a close connection between human beings, other organisms and habitats.

Tick the environments that make you feel happy.

1. Green parks ☐
2. Lakeside ☐
3. Small town ☐
4. Shopping malls ☐
5. Mountains ☐
6. Beaches ☐
7. Urban city ☐
8. Village ☐

Now, lets find out what we should do to conserve our natural environment.

1. Recycle everything you can.
2. Use cloth not paper napkins.
3. Use a pail and mug to bathe not a shower.
4. Use less heaters inside; wear a sweater.
5. Use waste to make compost.
6. Use reusable cups and dishes on a picnic.
7. Ride a cycle or walk instead of driving.
8. Print or write on both sides of the paper and don't use paper unnecessarily.
9. Plant trees and feed the birds.

Colour the poster. Circle with red the actions which waste water.

Solve the crossword with words connected to conservation using the given clues.

	1. G	2. A	T		O	S		H			E		3. W
	L												A
4. C		N	5. S		6. R	V			7. I	O			
	B												
					N				8. R	E			E
	L		A		E								
	W		R										
									A				
					B				T				
	M												
			9. G		E		N		O	U			
			10. S		S			I	N	A	B		
	G												

Across

2. A mixture of gases surrounding the earth
4. Protection of the natural environment
8. Using something again
9. A building with glass sides and a glass roof for growing plants
10. Economic development that is conducted without depletion of natural resources

Down

1. Increase in temperature of the earth's atmosphere caused by the increase of carbon dioxide
3. To use more of something than is necessary or useful
5. Connected with the sun
6. That which is replaced naturally
7. Supplying water to an area of land through pipes or channels so that crops will grow

Project I : Upcycle

Upcycling is the creative reuse of old or old products. Lets make a tote bag with a upcycled t-shirt.

Materials required

- An old T-shirt
- A pair of sharp scissors
- A marker pen

Method

1. Take and old t-shirt and fold it in half so that each sleeve falls exactly on the other. Cut both sleeves off neatly.

2. Turn the T-shirt inside out. Use the marker to draw a deep oval from one end of the neck to the other end. This is the mouth of your bag. Carefully cut along the marked line both the front and back of the T-shirt. You can use a bowl to draw the line.

3. Draw a horizontal line across the lower part of the front at least 4 inches from the bottom of the T-shirt.

4. Cut strips from the bottom of the T-shirt to the line. Each strip must be 1 inch apart. Cut the strips on the front and back of the shirt. Now there is a fringe at the bottom of the shirt.

5. Take your first pair of fringe and tie it into a knot, then tie two more pairs. Now if you lift your bag you'll see that although the pairs are pulling the bag together, there's a hole between each pair.

6. Look at the picture for this step and you will see three sets of fringe that have been tied in knots. Take one strand from the middle set and tie it in a knot with one of the strands on the left set. Then, take the other strand from the middle set and tie it in a knot with one of the strands on the right set.

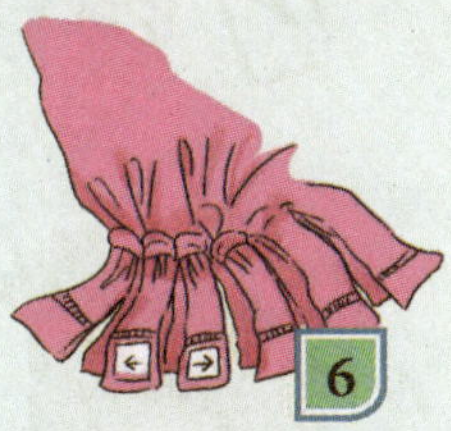

7. Then, take the remaining strand on the right set and tie it to the next set of strands, and so on and so forth until all the strands are tied. Now turn your T-shirt right side out. You have a beautiful tote bag from an old T-shirt.

Project II : Understanding Recycling

Answer these questions to find out more about recycling.

- What is recycling?
- How was the term coined?
- Recycling functions on the principle 'one person's trash is another person's treasure'. Explain this principle.
- Which are the different things one can recycle?
- Suggest two ways to recycle at home.
- Suggest two ways to recycle at school.
- Suggest two ways to recycle at workplace.
- Give the method to make an interesting recycle craft using trash items at school.
- Find out what are the civic authorities doing to promote recycling in your town, city or village.

7. Children Volunteers of Delhi

Discuss

Look at the pictures and discuss in class the rules being followed.

Obey the rule of queue.

Read along

Nation Times

Odd-Even Debut: Delhi Children Volunteers Lead The War

JAISHREE MURTHY

JAN 02, 2016, 3:14 IST

NEW DELHI: In a bid to cut smog in the world's most polluted capital, Delhi government launched its ambitious odd-even car scheme on Friday.

As the clock ticked 8 am on the first day of the New Year, traffic police personnel and civil defence volunteers could be seen implementing the odd-even vehicular restrictions on the city roads.

Among volunteers were many school children of the city. Students from various schools around the capital joined the Nation Times #Icantbreathe campaign, taking to the streets to assist traffic police in enforcing the pilot plan that will stay in force until January 15.

Speaking to Nation Times, Executive Director of Centre for Science and Environment, Anumita Sinha said, 'Children will form an important force in changing mindsets by motivating people to give up vehicles and use more public transport.'

Though on winter break, school students began the first day of the year holding placards, speaking to commuters about the benefits of cycling and carpooling.

To ensure safety of the children, a school staff member was asked to monitor their movements and the young volunteers were not allowed to venture out on the roads but remained positioned on the sidewalks.

Not only school children, but college students also actively participated in the drive. Students from Delhi University were seen on green cycles in a bid to inspire others to choose ecofriendly modes of transport.

While the Delhi government has announced that 6,000 more buses would hit city roads to make the odd-even drive a success, many people remain sceptical.

However, activist Harsh Mehta, on an optimistic note, applauded the students for their efforts to be agents of change.

Think and Say

You find the driver of your school bus driving rashly and jumping red traffic lights. What will you do?

Though the citizens of Delhi found it difficult to implement the rule of driving odd and even number registered cars on the days tagged for them, they obeyed the rule laid down by the government.

People pooled cars, used public transport and even cycled to work during this 15-day period. School and college children did their bit by adding their voices to that of the government and thus helped to reduce pollution in the city.

Despite personal problems, especially as the extensive expanse of the city meant long hours of travel, citizens of Delhi heeded these calls. Consequently, people in Delhi breathed a much better quality of air for those fifteen days. It is the duty of all citizens to respect rules made by the administration. Only then can they benefit from the facilities provided by the same administration.

We must remember that rights and duties go hand in hand.

Remember

- Without rules, there would be utter chaos. People would do anything they wanted, without any concern for others.
- Obey the rules because they were put in place to help make people as comfortable as possible.
- Laws can be made and unmade depending on the needs of a large number of people.
- Everybody must cooperate with rules. Only then there can be a good life for the maximum number of people.
- Everyone needs to work together to allow the society to function in a way that is as comfortable as possible for most people.

Figure out

A. Tick the correct answers.

1. Why did the school children help Delhi's police to implement the odd-even rule on the roads?
   a. It was fun to stop cars that did not obey rules. ☐
   b. They were eager to reduce the pollution in the city. ☐
2. Why would the motorists take the students' advice of cycling seriously?
   a. Motorists would be reminded that cycling reduced pollution. ☐
   b. Motorists would be reminded that most students cycle to their school. ☐
3. Although the Delhi government, police and students put in so much effort to make odd-even a success, why were people skeptical?
   a. They did not believe that the people of Delhi would co-operate. ☐
   b. They did not believe that the rule would reduce pollution. ☐
4. How did the people of Delhi react to the odd-even rule?
   a. They did not obey the rule. ☐
   b. They carpooled, used public transport and obeyed the rule. ☐
5. What is the duty of all citizens?
   a. They must obey all the rules made by the administration. ☐
   b. They must protest the rules that are otherwise fair and much needed. ☐

B. Explain with examples, the statement 'Rights and duties go hand in hand.'

Relate

Tick the best options for these situations.

1. You are late for a test and so your father is driving you to school. On the way, a police officer waves down the car. What will you do?
   a. tell your father to speed up and ignore the police officer ☐
   b. be patient and hope that the interaction will be brief ☐

2. You are the bus monitor and have the duty to see that everyone boards the bus in a disciplined way. What will you do?
   a. make everyone queue up to board the bus and get on yourself last ☐
   b. be the first to board, keep a seat for yourself and then discipline others ☐
3. The rule in your house is that everyone washes their plates after dinner. What will you do?
   a. leave your dirty plate in the sink and slip quietly slip into your room ☐
   b. wash your own plate and a few more dirty dishes to help your parents ☐
4. Students who are late for the morning assembly in your school are penalized. What will you do?
   a. go to your teacher when you are late and take the punishment quietly ☐
   b. enter from the back gate and slink off to your class whenever you are late ☐

Act

Classroom Rules

1. On a sheet of paper, write down five rules that are very important for students to follow in the classroom.
2. Form a pair with another student and discuss with your partner the rules that both of you have written down. Come up with two more rules that both of you think are important for the classroom.
3. With another pair of students, discuss the seven rules that each student among the four of you has written. Each of the four students should think of two more rules which would be important for the classroom.
4. Each group of four students will read their set of ten classroom rules in the class.

Happiness Box

1. **Make a poster on speaking rule and put it up in your room.**
   There are some important rules that we should follow before we start speaking. The most important one is to 'think before we speak'.

Before you speak

THINK!

Is it **T**rue?

Is it **H**elpful?

Is it **I**nspiring?

Is it **N**ecessary?

Is it **K**ind?

2. Role-play

Divide the class into teams of three students each. Two students pretend to speak to each other on the phone. While speaking, they break one rule of speaking on the phone. The third student should quote the correct rule after the role-play is over.

In the same group, give two rules for public speaking on stage while emceeing an event or presenting it. Discuss the rules given by all the groups in class.

Teaching tips

- Emphasize that rules must be followed even if it is inconvenient for people.
- Give simple examples to prove how confusion occurs without rules. You can describe the scene when traffic lights stop working on a busy intersection.
- Reiterate that nobody is above the rule or law. The penalty for everyone for breaking the rule is same.

8. Dorothy and the Scarecrow

Discuss

Look at the pictures and discuss in class the attitude of the students.

Read along

This extract from The Wizard of Oz is about a little Kansas farm girl, Dorothy Gale, and her dog Toto who are blown away in a tornado and left in a fairyland named Oz. There, she meets some memorable friends and foes in her journey to meet the Wizard of Oz who everyone says can help her return home.

Dorothy knew that only the Great Oz could help her get to Kansas again, so she bravely resolved not to turn back.

She started along the road of yellow brick. When she had gone several miles she thought she would stop to rest, and so climbed to the top of the fence beside the road and sat down. There was a great cornfield beyond the fence, and not far away, she saw a Scarecrow, placed high on a pole to keep the birds from the ripe corn.

Dorothy leaned her chin upon her hand and gazed thoughtfully at the Scarecrow.

Its head was a small sack stuffed with straw, with eyes, nose, and mouth painted on it to represent a face. An old, pointed blue hat that had belonged to some Munchkin was perched on his head, and the rest of the figure was a blue suit of clothes, worn and faded, which had also been stuffed with straw. On the feet were some old boots with blue tops, such as every man wore in this country, and the figure was raised above the stalks of corn by means of the pole stuck up its back.

While Dorothy was looking earnestly into the queer, painted face of the Scarecrow, she was surprised to see one of the eyes slowly wink at her. She thought she must have been mistaken at first, for none of the scarecrows in Kansas ever wink; but presently the figure nodded its head to her in a friendly way. Then, she climbed down from the fence and walked up to it, while Toto, the dog, ran around the pole and barked.

'Good day', said the Scarecrow, in a rather husky voice.

'Did you speak?' asked the girl, in wonder.

'Certainly', answered the Scarecrow. 'How do you do?'

'I'm pretty well', thank you', replied Dorothy politely. 'How do you do?'

'I'm not feeling well,' said the Scarecrow, with a smile, 'for it is very tedious being perched up here night and day to scare away crows.'

'Can't you get down?' asked Dorothy.

'No, for this pole is stuck up my back. If you will please take away the pole, I shall be greatly obliged to you.'

Dorothy reached up both arms and lifted the figure off the pole, for being stuffed with straw, it was quite light.

'Thank you very much,' said the Scarecrow, when he had been set down on the ground. 'I feel like a new man'.

Dorothy was puzzled at this, for it sounded queer to hear a stuffed man speak, and to see him bow and walk along beside her.

'Who are you?' asked the Scarecrow when he had stretched himself and yawned. 'And where are you going?'

'My name is Dorothy', said the girl, 'and I am going to the Emerald City, to ask the Great Oz to send me back to Kansas'.

'Where is the Emerald City?' he inquired. 'And who is Oz?'

'Why, don't you know?' she returned, in surprise.

'No, indeed. I don't know anything. You see, I am stuffed, so I have no brains at all,' he answered sadly.

'Oh', said Dorothy, 'I'm awfully sorry for you'.

'Do you think', he asked, 'If I go to the Emerald City with you, that Oz would give me some brains?'

'I cannot tell', she returned, 'But you may come with me, if you like. If Oz will not give you any brains, you will be no worse off than you are now.'

'That is true', said the Scarecrow. 'You see', he continued confidentially, 'I don't mind my legs and arms and body being stuffed, because I cannot get hurt. If anyone treads on my toes or sticks a pin into me, it doesn't matter, for I can't feel it. But I do not want people to call me a fool, and if my head stays stuffed with straw instead of brains, as yours is, how am I ever to know anything?'

'I understand how you feel', said the little girl, who was truly sorry for him. 'If you will come with me, I'll ask Oz to do all he can for you'.

'Thank you', he answered gratefully.

They walked back to the road. Dorothy helped him over the fence, and they started along the path of yellow brick for the Emerald City.

Toto did not like this addition to the party at first. He smelled around the stuffed man as if he suspected there might be a nest of rats in the straw, and he often growled in an unfriendly way at the Scarecrow.

'Don't mind Toto', said Dorothy to her new friend. 'He never bites'.

'Oh, I'm not afraid', replied the Scarecrow. 'He can't hurt the straw. Do let me carry that basket for you. I shall not mind it, for I can't get tired. I'll tell you a secret', he continued, as he walked along. 'There is only one thing in the world I am afraid of'.

'What is that?' asked Dorothy, 'the Munchkin farmer who made you?'

'No', answered the Scarecrow, 'It's a lighted match'.

—*Extracted from The Wonderful Wizard Of Oz by L.Frank Baum*

Saying 'No'

Personal Boundaries

Respect is thinking and acting positively about oneself and others. Respecting elders is a good habit, but we should not hesitate to say 'no' if someone asks you do something you aren't comfortable doing. Doing this should not be thought of as disrespect. We should place our safety before our manners. We can follow the rules and still respect ourselves and others. We can resist and report when someone breaks personal safety rules.

Remember

- We should meet people who are different from us.
- We must be tolerant towards things we dislike about others because there are things about us that others may dislike too.
- Be open to accepting people with different looks, ideas and opinions.
- Don't make prejudice a barrier to opening yourself to people.
- When you accept differences in people, they will accept your differences.
- Acceptance of people opens the doors to many opportunities, like friendship and travel.
- Everybody is entitled to their opinion and we should respect that right even if we don't necessarily agree with the opinion.

Figure out

A. Tick the correct answers.

1. Even though Dorothy found it strange that a scarecrow winked and nodded at her, why did she walk up to him?

   a. She wanted to find out whether she had imagined it. ☐

   b. She found the Scarecrow friendly. ☐

2. Why did Dorothy not ignore the scarecrow's request, even though it was unusual?
    a. Dorothy wanted to see the Scarecrow fall down without the pole supporting him. ☐
    b. Although the Scarecrow's request was unusual, Dorothy wanted to help him. ☐
3. What did Dorothy understand about the Scarecrow?
    a. The Scarecrow wanted a brain so that he could know about things. ☐
    b. The Scarecrow wanted a human body so that he could feel like a person. ☐
4. How did the Scarecrow help Dorothy?
    a. He showed her the way to Oz. ☐
    b. He carried the basket for Dorothy. ☐
5. Although Toto did not like him, why did Dorothy take him along with her?
    a. Dorothy was kind and accepted the Scarecrow despite his appearance and strange wishes. ☐
    b. Dorothy wanted to show the strange walking-talking Scarecrow to her friends. ☐

B. Elucidate the saying 'Be different! Don't walk with the herd'

Relate

Tick the best options for these situations.

1. A boy who lives in the slum behind the park has come to play in the park. What will you do?
    a. quickly move away from him because your friends may see you with him ☐
    b. invite him to be part of your gang ☐
2. Your house help's son has been wearing old and ragged clothes. What will you do?
    a. talk politely to him and see if you have a pair of trousers that fit him ☐
    b. make fun of his clothes ☐

3. The boy who tops the class in every test is the son of a rickshaw puller. What will you do?
   a. avoid talking or socializing with him
   b. congratulate him and ask him to help you with your studies
4. A classmate of yours starts crying every time he is scolded by a teacher. What will you do?
   a. console him by saying that teachers sometimes scold students
   b. laugh at him and call him a cry-baby
5. During the sports period, two of your classmates want to play basketball. Your team captain does not allow them as they are girls. What will you do?
   a. support the girls and ask the captain to let them play
   b. make fun of them and say girls cannot play

Act

Bursting Stereotypes

Keep a large number of small inflated balloons in a basket on a table along with strips of paper and some thumb pins. Work in pairs.

1. On a sheet of paper, each pair makes two columns—Boy, and Girl.
3. Each pair discusses and writes words they think describe a boy and a girl.
4. When each pair has finished the list, they should say the words aloud.
5. The class discusses whether each description is always true. If it is not, then it proves that it is a generalization and not true in every case.
6. Each student will then come to the table and write one stereotyped description about a man or a woman on a paper.
7. The student will ask the rest of the class whether this stereotyped view should be bursted.
8. When they agree, the student picks up a balloon and a pin from the basket, reads the description loudly and say, 'Burst!' and burst the balloon with the pin.

Happiness Box

I am Different

1. Every person is different and we have both good and bad qualities. There could be something about us that may seem unusual to others. Does that make you unacceptable to your friends?

Write five things that make you different in the picture below. Share it in your class.

2. Different yet Connected

a. Take four photographs of people who are very different from each other but have one thing that connects them.

b. Paste the photographs on a chart paper and write under each what makes that person different from the rest.

c. Below all the photographs, write what connects them.

Teaching tips

- Explain how being different is what makes each of us special.
- Reiterate that one must never be ashamed of one's different skin colour, religion, customs or region. Accept and be proud of these differences because they contribute to one's personality.
- Emphasize that including everyone socially makes for one's own inclusion in all groups.

9. Brave Arunima

Discuss

Read and discuss in class what these words mean.

'Each mistake teaches you something new about yourself. There is no failure, remember, except in no longer trying. It is the courage to continue that counts.'

—*Chris Bradford*

Read along

There are people who never let anything stand in their path when they make up their mind. Arunima Sinha is one of those people. In 2013, she became the first differently-abled person to climb Mt Everest. Those who know her have been extremely impressed by her courage and her motto of 'Never say Never'.

Today, Arunima is very satisfied that she has done what she had vowed herself she would. She had been a national level volleyball and football player until she met with an accident that changed her life completely. On 11 April 2011, she had boarded the Padmavati Express from Lucknow to Delhi. Arunima was going to the capital to take an examination to join the CISF. On the train, she was attacked by thieves who wanted to snatch her bag. Since she resisted, they threw her from the train. A train coming from the other side crushed her leg. Arunima was treated at a hospital, but her leg had to be amputated to save her life. For four months, she underwent treatment at the All India Institute of Medical Sciences where an Indian company gifted her with an artificial leg. Life looked very desolate to a person who had been extremely active and independent. While she was being treated, she came to know about Yuvraj Singh's battle with cancer. She decided that she, too, must do something, with her life. Then and there, she vowed to herself that she will climb Mt Everest.

In fact, her accident had changed the way Arunima thought. It was because she had lost her leg that she became adamant to climb Mt Everest. She wanted to prove to herself as well as to others that she was as strong as she had always been.

But being a sportsperson, Arunima realized she would need special training and build up her mental stamina. So she contacted Bachendri Pal and signed up to train under her. She had to work very hard. Sometimes, it was just too painful but she kept at it.

In 2012, Arunima climbed Island Peak in preparation for the climb to Mt Everest. It was in 2013 that she started the ascent of Mt Everest. It took her 52 days to reach the summit. The last leg of the climb was the toughest. It was a hard toil of 17 hours before Arunima stood on the summit at 10.55 am on 21 May, 2013. She felt ecstatic. It was a moment of pure joy for her that she could not express in words.

It had been a long and difficult struggle to realize her vow but she had refused to give up. Yet, when asked about her tremendous effort, Arunima prefers giving credit to the opportunity that Tata Steel Adventure Foundation gave her. She believed that the trainers and Bachendri Pal played a major role in preparing her physically and mentally for the climb.

Arunima returned to Lucknow to a hero's welcome by the chief minister and the sports minister of Uttar Pradesh. Since then, Arunima has received many accolades and awards. But that is not enough for her.

She has a dream and another goal to achieve. She wants to open a free sports academy for the poor and differently-abled people. All her award money as well as everything she earns from seminars is being poured into its creation. She has already bought a plot of land for it.

This Academy is a grand dream, but Arunima has realized that there is nothing one cannot do with perseverance. Her aim is to provide a platform through which differently-abled people can achieve their goals. She wants to make people who are differently-abled strong and independent through sports. While Arunima prays that God makes her dream a reality, nothing can stop a determined person and especially one who perseveres like her. We all expect that Arunima will succeed in this just like she succeeded in climbing Mt Everest.

Remember

- You only fail when you give up trying.
- Every failure teaches you what you should not do. They are the stepping stones to success.
- Always try to improve yourself when you fail.
- If you are focused on your goal, nothing can stop you.
- Be inspired by people who have overcome obstacles to succeed.

Figure out

A. Tick the correct answers.

1. Though it was due to Arunima Sinha's determination that she has been able to carry out her vow, why does she give credit to others for it?
   a. She wanted to please these people. ☐
   b. She knows that just determination is not enough, one needs the help of others to achieve something. ☐

2. Why did Arunima resist the thieves?

a. Because Arunima did not believe in giving up but in fighting against wrong actions.

b. Arunima was proud of her strength and wanted to prove that she could defeat the thieves.

3. Even though she had lost her leg, why was Arunima determined to climb Mt Everest?

a. She wanted to win awards as the first differently-abled person to climb Mt Everest.

b. She wanted to prove that it was possible for her to do anything despite having an artificial leg.

4. Though the training was tough, how did Arunima reach her goal?

a. The other climbers carried her to the summit of Mt Everest.

b. She persevered and refused to give up despite the pain and hard work.

5. Why does she want to build a sports academy specially for differently-abled people?

a. She wants to give the differently-abled people a platform to achieve their goals.

b. She wants to become the hero of the differently-abled community.

B. Write a speech for the morning assembly on the saying, 'Never say Never'.

Relate

Tick the best options for these situations.

1. You are a good actor and have always been selected for the class play. This year, another student who is also a good actor has been selected. What will you do?

a. decide never to act again

b. practise harder and get selected next year

2. You and your brother love rock climbing but there is a huge rock behind your house which your brother can climb but you cannot. What will you do?

a. keep trying to climb it until one day you reach the peak

b. say reaching its peak is not in your fate and give up

3. You want to be the best athlete in your school in the long jump event, but every time you try to break the last highest record set, you fail. What will you do?
   a. decide to change your sport and in that way achieve the position of best sportsman ☐
   b. keep on trying to improve your jump records to beat the highest record ☐

4. You participate in the cycling marathon but are unable to clock the correct time. What will you do?
   a. rant and rave and lose your temper ☐
   b. calmly cycle every morning to increase your stamina so as to clock correctly next time ☐

Act

Organize a Never-Give-Up week in class.

Every morning, take turns to either tell a brief story or narrate a personal experience about never giving up.

Happiness Box

NED Pledge

1. **Here is a pledge everyone must take.**

   Never give up　　**E**ncourage others　　**D**o your best

   Make a poster for the NED Pledge.

Materials required

- 8 × 11 inches paper in bright colours
- Coloured pens or markers
- Scissors and tape

Method

1. Look at the picture and make a poster like it.
2. Make a colourful border with the sentences of the NED pledge.
3. Inside the border, write the pledge and the names of the people who will take it such as yourself, your friends and family.

2. **Find the song, 'We Shall Overcome One Day' on the Internet. The entire class can learn it and sing it together.**

Teaching tips

- Ensure all students understand that failures are only a path to success.
- Emphasize that one should never fall prey to disappointment.
- Reiterate that one must always be self-confident and never lose faith in one's capabilities.

10. The Enchanted Shirt

Discuss

Read this statement and discuss its meaning in class.

> 'Let your smile change the world
> But don't let the world change your smile.'
> —*Connor Franta*

Read along

The King was sick. His cheeks were red
And his eyes were clear and bright
He ate and drank with a kingly zest,
And peacefully snored at night.

But he said he was sick, and a king should know,
And doctors came by the score.
They did not cure him. He cut off their heads
And sent to the schools for more.

At last two famous doctors came,
And one was as poor as a rat,
He had passed his life in studious toil,
And never found time to grow fat.

The other had never looked in a book;
His patients gave him no trouble,
If they recovered they paid him well,
If they died their heirs paid double.

Together they looked at the royal tongue,
As the King on his couch reclined;
In succession they thumped his august chest,
But no trace of disease could find.

The old sage said, 'You're as sound as a nut'.
'Hang him up' roared the King in a gale,
In a ten-knot gale of royal rage;
The other leech grew a shade pale;

But he pensively rubbed his sagacious nose,
And thus his prescription ran,
The King will be well, if he sleeps one night
In the Shirt of a Happy Man.

Wide o'er the realm the courtiers rode,
And fast their horses ran,
And many they saw, and to many they spoke,
But they found no Happy Man.

***

At last as they came to a village gate,
A beggar lay whistling there;
He whistled and sang and laughed and rolled
On the grass in the soft June air.

***

'This is our man', the courtier said;
'Our luck has led us aright.
I will give you a hundred ducats, friend,
For the loan of your shirt to-night'.

The merry blackguard lay back on the grass,
And laughed till his face was black;
'I would do it, God wot', and he roared with fun,
'But I haven't a shirt to my back'.

Each day to the King the reports came in
Of his unsuccessful spies,
And the sad panorama of human woes
Passed daily under his eyes.

And out he went in the world and toiled
In his own appointed way;
And the people blessed him, the land was glad,
And the King was well and gay.

—John Hay

Think and Say

When you go out to play, you often quarrel with your friends. So you stay indoors but that gives you a headache. What will you do?

Remember

- Making others happy brings contentment.
- Spending energy and effort on others makes us strong.
- Listening to others' problems sometimes provides solutions to our problems.
- Spread joy with little words of kindness.
- Bringing a smile to a sad face brings sunshine into our own lives.
- Always see if there is some way to help the have-nots.

Figure out

A. Tick the correct answers.

1. Though he looked healthy, the King
   a. said that he was sick. ☐
   b. could not walk fast. ☐
2. The king was angry and punished the doctors
   a. who gave him many medicines. ☐
   b. when they could not find any disease in his body. ☐
3. The King sent his courtiers to get him
   a. the shirt of a happy man which would cure him. ☐
   b. a special flower which was the medicine for his disease. ☐
4. His courtiers brought him
   a. many shirts from the happy people in his kingdom. ☐
   b. no shirt, only news of the unhappy people in his kingdom. ☐
5. The search for the shirt made the King realize that
   a. except him, everybody in his kingdom was well and happy. ☐
   b. people in his kingdom needed his care to be well and happy. ☐

B. The beggar who did not even have a shirt was happier and healthier than the King with all his wealth. Give your reasons why this was so.

Relate

Tick the best options for these situations given below.

1. When you visit your sick friend, you find her very sad. What will you do?
   a. add to her sadness by telling her about all the studies she is missing ☐
   b. cheer her up by telling her about the good things at school that day ☐
2. You are the captain of your football team and want to win the match. What will you do?
   a. always find faults with your team and make them unhappy and nervous ☐
   b. always encourage your team and help the weaker ones ☐
3. Your grandfather lies in bed all the time and complains of aches and pains. What will you do?
   a. ignore him and go about your activities ☐
   b. find out about his interests and encourage him to join all family activities ☐
4. You have a neighbour who has to be in the wheelchair and looks sad. What will you do?
   a. pass him by and run for your basketball practice ☐
   b. talk to him and greet him politely ☐

Act

Teaching Empathy

Empathy is the ability to understand and share each other's feelings.

Make five groups in the class, and each group will adopt a class from the primary school.

Each group will make notes reminding its adopted class how to treat their classmates with empathy, that is, kindness and helpfulness to spread cheer. Put the notes up on the display board of the adopted class and talk to the students about how they should behave.

Listen to Your Friend.

Happiness Box

1. Make a poster for your room as given here. It will remind you of the ways you can add happiness to the lives of your classmates, siblings, parents and friends.

H = **Happiness**

A = **Appreciation**

P = **Passion and Strength**

P = **Perspective**

I = **Inner friend**

N = **Nudge out sadness**

E = **Empathy**

S = **Silently listen**

S = **Share your gifts**

2. **Look at this Mathematics of Life.**

MATHEMATICS OF LIFE

Life + Love = **Happy**

Life – Love = **Sad**

$$2 \text{ Life} = \text{Happy} + \text{Sad}$$

$$\therefore \text{Life} = \frac{\text{Happy} + \text{Sad}}{2}$$

$$\therefore \text{Life} = \tfrac{1}{2} \text{ Happy} + \tfrac{1}{2} \text{ Sad}$$

That's Real Life. Enjoy It.

Make a similar equation for Mathematics of Happiness.

Teaching tips

- Emphasize on the fact that making others happy makes one happy.
- Reiterate emotional contentment gives physical wellness.
- Remind students that a positive mind creates positivity around it.

11. Robin Hood

Discuss

Look at the pictures and discuss in class how rights and responsibilities go together.

I have the right to protest

I am responsible for law and order.
I protest peacefully.

Read along

Sir Robert of Locksley makes an enemy of the Norman noble, Sir Guy of Gisbourne and is forced to turn outlaw. Sir Guy orders the Sheriff of Nottingham to capture Sir Robert, who now calls himself Robin Hood. He and his band of Merry Men rob from the rich, give to the poor, hoodwink the Sheriff and foil the eff orts of the cruel Sir Guy.

From the shelter of the tree behind which he stood, Locksley saw three wardens appear out of the shadows not far behind Will who was running. They were so silent on their feet that Will had no idea that they were closing on him.

In the time it took the three men to halve the distance between themselves and the poacher. Robert had moved to where he had seen Will drop his bow. He had already taken the decision which would shape the rest of his life.

He knew what would happen to Will if caught and he knew what would happen to the children too, if their father ended the day on the end of a rope.

In the time it took him to make the ten strides to the bow, he knew what he must do.

In a flash, he had the bow in his hand, an arrow notched to the bowstring and two arrows ready on the ground next to him. He looked up to find that two of the men had seized Will by the arms and were holding him as he struggled to break free.

Think and Say

Your class monitor is very strict. He penalizes all those who break rules but not if they are his friends. What will you do?

Robert took the man on the left, pulled back the string and let go. The arrow flew straight, silent and true, thudding into the back of the man. By the time, the other wardens realized what was happening, the second arrow was already winging its way towards the man on the right, and less than three seconds after the first man fell, the second was clutching at his neck as an arrow pierced his body just below the shoulder.

But the third man was behind Will, and Robert did not dare shoot at him.

'Will, get down, get down, Let me see him,' shouted Robert. But the third man was already scampering away through the trees to safety and the office of the Abbot.

By the time Robert joined Will, the other two wardens had breathed their last. Will seemed rooted to the ground with fear, unable to move or speak.

'Will, come on, we have to get away from here! There are more of them in the forest for sure. Take out your knife, cut from the animal what you can carry and let's be gone.'

Their luck was in as they moved silently towards Will's home. Once they felt they were on safer ground, they began to talk. 'You are a fool to risk your life alone like this, Will Scarlet,' Robert began.

'If you had been caught . . .'
'So what do we do then? You have no idea. Your land is safe, you are a freeman and respected for your brave deeds in the King's army. Who am I? Nobody. Nothing. They know nothing of me and hundreds like me. They feed their hounds better and care more for horses than they do for their tenants and servants. They use the law of the land against us however they wish and ignore it whenever it doesn't suit them.'

They walked on in silence, and then Robert spoke, 'You're wrong Scarlet. I have just thrown away all I had by saving you from the Sheriff 's rope.

The alarm has been raised by now and before sunset they'll be looking for me . . . and you too.

Robert stood by the edge of the wood at the point where the path to his home broke off from the main track. He stood still, gazing in the distance.

'If they treat the law with such little respect and treat those who try to live by the law with so little care, then perhaps it's time for lesser folk to do likewise. Bad laws are worse than no laws at all. It's time we took back what belongs to us, what is rightfully ours.'

Locksley turned his eyes away from the path home, looked along the other track and began to walk.

'I believe my path lies in this direction now, he said firmly. 'Are you with me, Will? We are many, they are few. We have cunning, guile, knowledge of this land and these woods. And these woods can support us. They are rich with food, enough for many to live on and when times become harder, there will be some who pass by that have more than they need'.

Robert paused to see what his companion had to say, but when there was no response, he continued, his enthusiasm growing with every stride along the path.

'We will never take more than we need to live, not like those who rule us. Fairness and equality will be our watchwords, not greed and injustice. We will help our people find a new way to live. They'll come after us but we use the woodlands to shelter us, to hide us, to protect us as well as any armour. If they want us, then they will have to brave the forest to find us. And we will be waiting'.

And Robert of Locksley was true to his word. Thus, Robin Hood was born.

Remember

- Everybody has the right to be treated with respect and dignity.
- People have the right to not be hurt by others' careless and dangerous behaviour.
- All students have the right to to go to school and receive education.
- Everyone has the right to explain their own behaviour in a civil manner and be listened to.
- You have the responsibility of not hurting anyone by your careless and dangerous behaviour.
- You have the responsibility to ensure that school is a pleasant place.
- You have the responsibility to listen courteously when others speak.

Figure out

A. Tick the correct answers.

1. Why were the three wardens running after Will?
   a. Will had poached an animal in the King's forests and that was against the law. ☐
   b. The wardens were running a race with Will. ☐
2. The wardens were running a race with Will.
   a. Locksley decided to shoot Will down. ☐
   b. Locksley decided to defend Will. ☐
3. Does Will believe it is right to break the law?
   a. No, he is forced to poach because the King and his men do not look after poor men like him. ☐
   b. Yes, he likes to steal from the King's men. ☐
4. Why does Robert Locksley decide to protect Will even though he is breaking the law?
   a. Locksley takes this decision because he did not want to support bad laws. ☐
   b. Locksley takes this decision because he was Will's best friend. ☐
5. According to Locksley what will be the principles of his group?
   a. To steal, destroy and break all laws. ☐
   b. Fairness, equality and to never take more than they need. ☐

B. Describe an incident that ends with these words, 'I have just thrown away all I had by saving you'.

Relate

Tick the best options for these situations.

1. Your school is electing the school prefects through student votes. What will you do?
   a. be eager to vote as it is your right and your responsibility to see that your school has a good panel of prefects ☐
   b. stay at home as you find the voting process a waste of time ☐

2. You are not the bus monitor, but you notice that some younger students have their arms out of the windows. What will you do?

   a. not bother because it is not your responsibility ☐

   b. ensure that the students sit properly as their safety is your responsibility ☐

3. You are tidying your room, and the dustbin is overflowing with all the waste. What will you do?

   a. bin it for reuse and recycling as conservation is your responsibility too ☐

   b. dump it in the common area as you don't care about conservation ☐

4. You realize that you are cycling on the wrong side of the road. What will you do?

   a. quickly change lanes because you don't want to break the law ☐

   b. remain in the incorrect lane as it is daring to break laws ☐

Act

Organize a community drive in your school

Divide your class into groups. Give each group activities to improve your school. The activities could be planting trees, fundraising through jumble sale, picking up trash, donations for sports equipment that the whole school can use.

Invite your families and friends to participate in the activity your group is organizing. It will be fun, and you will feel responsible in giving your school community a facility that they will enjoy.

Happiness Box

1. **Make badges for your group as well as the families and friends participating in school community drive. They will love to be identified as a helper for the community work they are doing.**

   Materials required

   - Felt
   - Sheet of stiff coloured cartridge
   - Glue
   - Markers
   - Safety pins

Method

1. Cut the sheet of cartridge sheet and the felt into rectangles of 3 × 2 inches.
2. Paste the felt and the paper with glue.
3. Make a decorative border on the paper.
4. Write on the badge with coloured markers: I am a community helper. Write about what you have done to help someone.
5. Pin the badge to the shirt by attaching the felt to the shirt with a safety pin.

2. Write a 4-line verse titled *My Rights*.

Teaching tips

- Emphasize that everybody has been granted similar rights by the constitution and all have the right to enjoy them.
- It is everyone's duty to ensure that others fully avail their rights regardless of age, social status or class.
- Clearly reiterate the rights of students.

12. Le Chambon

Discuss

Look at the pictures and discuss in class what the boy in the car is doing.

Read along

During the times when the Nazis dominated most of Europe, when millions of Jews were being torn from their communities and sent off to the death camps, there was a village of three thousand farmers who decided to take the responsibility to provide sanctuary to Jewish refugees until they could be spirited to safety. For four years, the villagers of Le Chambon in France risked their lives defending innocent people against the Nazis. The refugees were not a small number. It was estimated that there were twenty-five hundred Jews, mostly children, who had been rescued.

Of course, the government was well aware of Le Chambon's efforts. The village was not far from the French capital of Vichy. The officials from there made a number of determined efforts to get the villagers to surrender their guests. They sent policemen and buses to Le Chambon but the villagers refused to cooperate with the police and hid the refugees. Finally, a day came when the Nazis took direct control of the region. The Gestapo conducted a raid and caught a few children, whom they deported, along with the families sheltering them, to the death camps. The Gestapo also caught and sentenced

Dr Roger Le Forestier, a local leader, to death as an example to the villagers. But even with a threat to their lives and their families' lives, the villagers refused to give up their guests.

In fact, the raw courage displayed by the villagers helped to change the minds and move the hearts of many of their opponents. The Vichy government slowly gave up efforts to carry out the Nazi directives. Later, the German military commander of the region, Major Schmehling, influenced by Dr Le Forestier's moving speech at his trial, tried to explain to the Gestapo chief, Colonel Metzger, the futility of fighting the villagers. He said, 'I told Metzger that this kind of resistance had nothing to do with violence, nothing to do with anything we could destroy with violence'. But Metzger was not convinced and insisted that Schmehling use strong tactics to flush out the hidden refugees. Schmehling kept using a delaying strategy, and eventually France was liberated. The lives of the Jewish refugees and that of the brave villagers of Le Chambon were saved.

Why should the villagers have cared so much to risk their lives for a group of strangers? When asked this question decades later, Roger Darcissac, a local pastor, explained, 'It all happened very simply. We didn't ask ourselves why. Because it's the human thing to do something like that. That's all I can tell you'.

An elderly peasant echoed his explanation, saying, 'Because we were human, that's all'.

Remember

- Always treat people with kindness and generosity.
- Help people in need.
- Be sensitive to people's feelings.
- Never be mean or hurtful.
- Think how your actions will affect others.
- We can become caring people by doing caring things for others.

Figure out

A. Tick the correct answers.

1. Why did the villagers of Le Chambon give shelter to the Jewish refugees?

   a. The Nazis were deporting the Jews to death camps. ☐

   b. The villagers wanted to play a match with the refugees. ☐

2. Why were the authorities determined to make the villagers give up the Jews?
   a. It was against the Nazi law to protect Jews.
   b. The authorities wanted to take the Jews to their homes.
3. Even when the Gestapo executed their leader, why did the villagers refuse to cooperate with the authorities?
   a. The villagers were criminals and wanted to break the law.
   b. The Nazi law of killing people just because they were Jews was inhuman.
4. How did this act of bravely caring for the refugees influence the others?
   a. The others laughed at the villagers for taking foolish risks.
   b. The others were impressed by the villagers who continued doing what was right despite risks.
5. Why could the villagers' resistance not be destroyed by violence?
   a. The villagers' resistance came from their conviction that being human, it was their duty to care and protect other humans.
   b. The villagers had more weapons than the Nazi forces did.

B. Write a story that shows caring people help others not because they expect a reward but because it is natural to show kindness.

Relate

Tick the best options for the situations given below.

1. You want to be friends with a new student in your class but the leader of your gang orders not to do so. What will you do?
   a. obey the leader as you are afraid of him
   b. refuse to obey the leader as you believe it is right for you to be friends with the new student
2. Your brother breaks his cricket bat accidently. At home your father scolds him for his carelessness. What will you do?
   a. stand up for your brother and tell your father it was not his fault
   b. remain silent as you are afraid your father will scold you too

3. You see a little kitten being attacked by a ferocious dog. What will you do?
   a. run to the kitten to protect it even though the dog may attack you ☐
   b. run far away because the dog may attack you ☐
4. You see a child drowning in a flooded river and you are strong swimmer. What will you do?
   a. ignore the child because swimming in a flooded river is dangerous ☐
   b. dive into the river because saving the child is foremost on your mind ☐

Act

Enact Story

Here is a brief story. Form groups and act out the story for the rest of the class.

Once a very rich boy was gifted a mirror. He hung it in his room, but it was strange that whenever he looked into it he found his face had a sad expression. He tried smiling or laughing, but the face in the mirror remained sad. He ate his favourite ice cream and felt happy. Yet, when he looked into the mirror he saw the same sad face looking back. One day, in the park, the rich boy found a little girl crying. When he asked her what the matter was, she said she had lost her parents. So the boy held her hand and started looking for her parents. The girl kept crying. So the boy bought her some sweets. Still, she would not stop crying. Finally, they found her parents. The boy was satisfied that he could help the little girl. That night, when he looked into the mirror, he found his reflection smiling back at him.

Happiness Box

1. **I CARE Pen Holder**

Materials required

- Empty, clean plastic cylindrical container
- Scrapbook papers: One solid colour and one patterned
- Ribbon
- Glue
- Coloured markers and stickers

Method

1. Start by cutting the solid colour paper sheet to the height of the container.

2. Stick the solid colour paper sheet onto the outer surface of the empty container.
3. Cut the patterned sheet half the height of the container and stick it on the solid colour sheet but only on the bottom half of the container.
4. Apply glue to one side of the ribbon and wrap it on the upper and lower edge of the patterned paper all around the container. Let the cut off edges overlap and apply a little dot of glue to stick them firmly together.

Use coloured markers to write ' I C♥RE' all around the container and place stickers all around it.

Keep it on your desk to stand your pens.

2. Play Charades with Care Words

1. Form two groups in your class.
2. Each group will silently act out a word related to the word CARE.
3. The other group will have to guess the word.
4. Each correct guess gives the team one point. The team with the most points wins.
5. Some words related to CARE are help, guide, console, responsibility, concern, blessing, comfort, calm. You may add more.

Teaching tips

- Explain that feelings of concern cannot be accompanied by any expectations.
- Caring is beneficial to the giver as well as the receiver. It brings happiness to both.
- No act of caring is too small. So don't hesitate to show that you care by words and actions.

Goal 7: Affordable and Clean Energy

- Millions of people do not have access to electricity.
- Thousands of people lack clean cooking fuels and rely on wood, charcoal, coal or animal waste for cooking and heating.
- Energy is the dominant contributor to climate change, accounting for around 60 per cent of global greenhouse gas emissions.

Take A Stand!

Use renewable sources of energy that neither pollute nor harm the earth.

Never waste precious natural resources like water and electricity.

Explore alternative sources of energy that enable you to go off-grid.

Clean Energy

- Solar energy is the energy we get from the sun's heat and light.
- Solar panels harness the sun's energy. They can be used in homes, offices to produce heat and electricity.
- Solar energy can power small devices like calculators and wristwatches and even automobiles like cars and buses.

> The Earth receives more energy from the Sun in an hour than the entire world uses in a year!

- Hydropower or hydroelectricity refers to the conversion of energy from flowing water into electricity.
- A hydroelectric power plant can supply large amounts of electricity which can be adjusted per demand.

- Wind energy is harnessed by wind turbines to generate electricity.
- Modern shipping companies use wind energy to reduce fuel consumption by installing large kites.

- Geothermal energy is the power generated from the Earth's internal heat.
- Many buildings use geothermal heat pumps to cool and heat buildings.
- Geothermal power plants use the energy from steam or hot water to drive turbines that produce electricity.

> Geothermal power facilities generate 25 per cent of Iceland's total energy production!

Project III : Our Unsung Heroes

Look at how an autorickshaw driver in Delhi helps to unite lost children with their parents.

Find out more about an autorickshaw driver in New Delhi who has attached himself to the police and embarked on a mission to unite lost children with their family.

Make a project report on another such citizen who helps the society.

Project IV : Unsung Heroes

1. There were many more people who are known for their immense contribution to humanity, both in India and abroad. Find out more about the unsung heroes listed here and write a project report on their contributions. You may write about any other unsung hero too.
    - Mary Anning
    - Gulabi Gang
    - Dr Megan Coffee
    - Prof. Hidayet Saiyed
    - Seema Rao

2. Write about a real-life unsung hero you know. Paste his or her picture too.